THIS BOOK IS FOR

BORN

LOTS OF LOVE
FORVER & ALWAYS

Made in the USA
San Bernardino, CA
24 June 2020

73995089R00086